ANUBIS SPEAKS!

SECRETS OF THE ANCIENT GODS

ANUBIS SPEAKS!

A GUIDE TO THE AFTERLIFE BY THE EGYPTIAN GOD OF THE DEAD

VICKY ALVEAR SHECTER
ILLUSTRATED BY ANTOINE REVOY

BOYDS MILLS PRESS
AN IMPRINT OF HIGHLIGHTS
Honesdale, Pennsylvania

The author wishes to thank Kasia Szpakowska, PhD, Senior
Lecturer in Egyptology, Department of History & Classics, Centre for
Egyptology & Mediterranean Archaeology (CEMA), Swansea University,
Wales, and Janice Kamrin, PhD, Assistant Curator, Department of
Egyptian Art, Metropolitan Museum of Art, for their valuable assistance
in the preparation of this book. In addition, she would like to thank her
wonderful editor, Larry Rosler, for believing in Anubis and refusing to let
him go quietly into the dark night.

Boyds Mills Press, Inc.
815 Church Street
Honesdale, Pennsylvania 18431
Printed in China
ISBN: 978-1-59078-995-7
Library of Congress Control Number: 2013938853
First edition
10 9 8 7 6 5 4 3 2 1
The text for this book is set in Century Schoolbook and
Gill Sans STD.
The illustrations are done in pen and ink and ink wash.

To my family, for putting up with my endless stories
—VAS

To Michelle Aimée Revoy Morel, who read the myths
of ancient Egypt to her sons
—AR

CONTENTS

CAUTION

ANUBIS WOULD LIKE TO advise you that his retelling of Ra's journey through the Land of the Dead combines stories from various papyri and tomb paintings that make up the *Books of the Afterlife*, such as the *Book of Caverns*, *Book of Hours*, *Book of Hidden Chambers*, *Book of Gates*, and others. He knows that ancient Egyptian stories and beliefs often changed by district or dynasty and that they often contradicted one another. He selected the stories that he thought best captured the gist of ancient Egyptian beliefs, and also the ones that had the highest chance of scaring you and grossing you out.

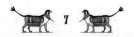

GREETINGS, MORTAL

ALLOW ME TO INTRODUCE MYSELF. I am
Anubis—the Egyptian god of the "Mysteries of
Embalming," the "Guardian of the Veil of Death,"
"Opener of the Ways of the Dead," and if you are
"bad" . . . *Your. Worst. Nightmare.*

But do not fear. I will not snatch your beating
heart from your chest and toss it to my good friend,
crocodile-headed Amut the Destroyer, for a squishy
snack . . . not *today* anyway. Instead, I will guide you
through my world of deep magic, strange gods, and
gruesome monsters. I will show you how my people,
the ancient Egyptians, prepared the dead for eternal
life, and how we gods fought the forces of darkness

and evil—every night—to keep you safe.

Oh dear, were you perhaps hoping for a less scary-looking guide to lead you through the Egyptian dark lands, one without so many razor-sharp fangs? Too bad. You're in my realm now. And I'm in charge. So pay attention.

We will, soon enough, come face-to-face with the evil one—Apophis, the snake of doom that threatens to devour and destroy the world. In my day, only our dead pharaohs—kings who turned into immortal gods upon their deaths—were strong enough to join the rest of us gods in facing the beast.

You, my little human, are no pharaoh, but I'm allowing you to come along anyway. You may thank me later, preferably in buckets of blood. Meanwhile, take heed; if you scare easily, I suggest you close this book right now and go back to coloring rainbows and unicorns.

Seriously.

There will be blood. And snakes. And decapitations. And monsters who like to gobble up hearts and squeeze heads until they pop.

Still with us?

Good. Then, please, step into my lair. . . .

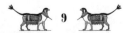

THE DARK LANDS

WELCOME TO DUAT, the Egyptian afterworld. It's a little dark, yes, but what did you expect? This world only comes alive after the sun sets . . . and after you die, of course (not like I'm looking forward to that or anything).

The Egyptian Land of the Dead was sometimes called the "Twelve Hours of Darkness" for the long hours of the night. You see, my people believed that the sun was born every morning in the east at sunrise. When it disappeared in the west at sunset, they worried that evil in the dark lands would keep the sun from rising again. Without the sun, everyone and everything would die! So it became really, really

important to make sure that the sun survived.

The sun's survival and rebirth also became a powerful metaphor for the individual's rebirth in the afterworld.

Lots of gods and monsters played a role in this battle between light and dark, death and eternal life. You will meet some of them on this journey. Keep in mind, there are thousands of us gods. Not only that, but the same god could appear in many different forms! So you won't get to know all of us, which is fine because really, I'm the only one that matters.

THE PEOPLE WHO WORSHIPPED US

The ancient Egyptians first settled near the fertile banks of the Nile River around five thousand years ago. Over time they banded together to form one kingdom under the rule of pharaohs that lasted for thousands of years. (Yeah, and how long has your nation been around? Mortal, *please*. It doesn't even come close to matching our longevity!)

My people invented a type of writing called hieroglyphics. They created the first paper from papyrus. They established a calendar that became the basis for the Western calendar. And they built great pyramids, statues, and temples that continue to awe humans around the world today. In other words,

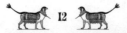

while you folks in the West were just learning to walk without dragging your knuckles on the ground, my people created one of the richest and most advanced cultures of the ancient world.

You're welcome.

MAGIC AND MAYHEM

For the Egyptians, the world was a magical place where destruction and chaos could only be managed or avoided by a strict adherence to ritual, order, and worship. Praying to and honoring the gods were the glue that held Egyptian culture together. And it worked, too.

I should know.

But while we gods were the spiritual heart of the kingdom, the Nile River was its main artery.

THE GIFT OF THE NILE

The Greek writer Herodotus called Egypt "The Gift of the Nile." He was right. The Nile is like a thin thread of life in a wasteland of desert. The deserts on either side of the Nile, which Egyptians called the "red lands," provided a natural barrier from attack by invaders. The "black lands" of the Nile referred to the rich soil left on the banks after its annual flooding or inundation. Thanks to the fertility of the black lands, Egypt became known as

the breadbasket of the ancient world. The Nile was also the primary means of transportation, trade, and travel.

The great river was an important symbol of my people's religion, too. It separated east from west—east, where the sun was born, and west, where it set into the dark lands. Most mummies were buried on the west side of the Nile—in the red lands—in honor of this division. Most dead pharaohs took a symbolic journey on the Nile. Their bodies were carried on a funeral barge as they traveled to their eternal tombs.

With as much as my people owed the Nile, it's no surprise that their creation stories featured life-giving waters. There are three primary Egyptian creation myths, all beginning with the dark, primeval waters of Nun (or abyss). I will only tell you the one story that is related to *me* because, of course, it's the only one that matters.

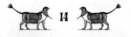

Egyptian Creation Myth
from the City of the Sun

IN THE BEGINNING, there was nothing but an endless swirling sea of chaos known as the dark primeval waters of Nun. The god Atum-Re (also known as Atum-Ra or Ra) willed himself into existence. He wanted to stand on something so he created a hill, which the Egyptians called Iunu, and the Greeks called Heliopolis (City of the Sun).

Atum brought light to the world by becoming a Bennu bird (heron). The Bennu bird perched on the hill and let out a honk so great, it called existence into being.

But Atum was lonely, so with a mighty glob of spit and snot he created his children, Shu, the god of air, and Tefnut, the goddess of moisture and water.

Shu and Tefnut had children of their own—Geb, god of the earth, and Nut, goddess of the sky. Geb lay down on the surface of the water, creating land. Nut arced over him, shining with light during the day and twinkling with stars at night.

Nut and Geb had four children: Isis, Osiris, Set, and Nephthys. The Egyptians called all of these gods, including Atum-Re, the Pesdjet, the Nine, or in Greek, the Ennead of Heliopolis—the first gods of Egypt.

How is this story related to me? Two of these

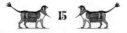

first gods, Osiris and Nephthys, are my parents.
That alone makes them worthy of special worship,
don't you think?

UNDERSTANDING RA (SOMETIMES CALLED ATUM), THE GOD WHO CREATED THE WORLD BY HOCKING A GIANT LOOGIE

Protecting Ra from the monster Apophis is why
we are here, folks. And yes, I agree that it's a
little undignified to know we all came from what
Ra spit up when he was bored. But still, we owe him,
right?

My people told many stories about Ra, the creator
god, but the following one is my favorite because it
features so much human death and destruction. And
blood. Lots and lots of human blood (*mmmm*, my
favorite snack). Plus it explains why Ra left us so he
could travel alone across the sky as the sun, or what
we called the sun disk.

And why, you may ask, did Ra refuse to continue
walking among his creations on earth? Because you
humans had to go and ruin it for the rest of us. You
plotted against him. You rebelled, thinking to steal
Ra's power (as if) for yourself.

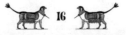

16

Ra withdrew into the sky in response to your sacrilege. So it's all your fault, you petty, backstabbing, power-hungry, smelly little mortals.

But I'm not resentful.

Really, I'm not.

Ra's Bloody Revenge

RA RULED ALL THAT HE CREATED, including gods and humans. But Ra grew old and tired. His bones became silver, his flesh gold, and his hair lapis lazuli. Some humans thought he was too old to rule. They wanted his power and plotted against him.

Furious, Ra called a secret meeting of the gods. "How should I punish those who plot to overthrow me?" the great god thundered.

Nun of the watery abyss advised him to get rid of the rebels. For good.

So Ra sent the goddess Hathor after them. She normally presented herself as a kindly, milk-giving cow. But Hathor also had a vengeful angry side known as Sekhmet, the lion-headed goddess.

Sekhmet pounced on the human evildoers who had fled to the desert. With a mighty roar, she devoured them and lapped up their blood before it could sink into the desert sands. Sekhmet discovered she relished the taste of human blood. She wanted more . . . and more.

She began to stalk good people, too; those who honored Ra and would never have plotted against him.

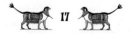

But Ra was not a vengeful god. He did not want all of humankind destroyed. He called Sekhmet back. But with the blood matting the fur on her face, she only roared, "Mmmmm, good. More! Must have more human blood!" And off she went on the hunt again. She vowed to keep hunting until all of humanity was destroyed.

Ra had to do something to stop her, so he came up with a plan. He sent his fastest messengers to gather the reddest clay they could find, bright red dirt called ochre. He ordered his servants to brew seven thousand clay jars of beer, and then he had the red ochre mixed in with the drink. As Sekhmet slept, Ra's servants emptied all seven thousand jars of beer into a field before her. She awoke to what seemed like a lake of blood and pounced on it, gulping it down.

But soon she grew full and woozy. After one mighty belch, she lay down to sleep. When she awoke she saw the remnants of the "blood" lake and thought, "My work here is done. I have killed all the humans in the world."

Her rage gone, Sekhmet turned back into Hathor, the placid divine cow, and returned to Ra. Ra was happy to have Hathor back, but he continued to resent humans for plotting against him. After all, if they had done so once, they would likely do so again.

"I am old and tired," Ra announced. "I wish to sink back into the waters of Nun until I am ready to be born again." He wanted to undo all that he had created!

So Nun called upon the sky goddess Nut to help Ra. Nut transformed into a cow with golden flanks and gilded horns, and told Ra to climb on her back. He did so and she carried him high into the heavens. But Nut grew dizzy at the height of the sun, and Ra called upon many gods, including Shu, the god of air, to support her as she supported him.

Removing himself to the heavens during the day meant Ra also traveled to the underworld at night to do battle with Apophis, the spirit of darkness and chaos. The people of earth, however, were frightened by the darkness and called out to Ra.

"I will provide light until I am born again," Ra announced. "I appoint Thoth as my assistant on earth." Ra commanded Thoth to provide some light during the dark hours. Thoth, then, came to represent the moon, as well as wisdom.

Ra always returned at dawn with the sunrise, though he never again mixed with the people and world he created.

Remember, young mortal, it was you humans and your greedy grasping that led to Ra's departure. So keep it under control while you're with me, or else. . . .

THE JOURNEY BEGINS

IT'S SHOWTIME, PEOPLE! Are you ready? The
time has come to climb into Ra's boat to join him on
his twelve-hour night journey and fight Apophis. It's
still not too late to change your mind. You could close
this book *right now* and go on your merry way.

But if you stay, don't blame me if you have
nightmares—especially about our enemy, Apophis,
the giant snake that is determined to destroy us. The
monster that slithers up from the swampy depths
of pure evil. To wait for you. *Under your bed.* (Just
kidding—about the under-your-bed part, anyway).

Apophis gave my people nightmares. He embodied
every slimy, scary, dark, miserable, uncontrollable evil

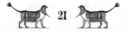

they could imagine.

We ancients didn't fool around when it came to Apophis.

And neither should you.

THE CAVERNS OF MISERY
≳ HOUR ONE ≳

See those baboons over there by the entrance to the first cavern? They are singing to welcome Ra into the underworld, just as they welcome him into the land of the living at sunrise. My people thought baboons spoke the secret language of the gods because they gathered together to chatter excitedly every day at both sunrise and sunset. They were the first to adore the sun god, my people believed, which was why baboons were often depicted as Thoth, the god of wisdom, or painted with their arms outstretched, adoring the sun.

When it came to adoring Ra, they didn't monkey around.

ENTERING THE DARK LANDS

This first hour of our journey is the period between twilight and night. Ra enters the dark lands in his solar boat, also known as the *Mandjet* or day boat. My people depicted the solar boat as looking like the pharaoh's royal barge—a long, thin, elegant ship often finished with precious metals and decorated at

each end with carved, painted papyrus plants.

Look, Ra is entering the first cavern. He appears exhausted, doesn't he? And with good reason, too. It's been a long, draining day, people. The sun god has made his slow journey through the twelve hours of the day, blessing all of Egypt with his light and energy. He has shined down on farmers tilling land, fishermen pulling in nets, masons carving massive temple stones, and children playing with wooden toys. During the transition between day and night, my people called Ra "Flesh" or "Auf" (corpse) because this was the hour he faded away, leaving the world in darkness.

TERROR IN THE NIGHT

Remember, we didn't have night lights and street lights like you moderns. When it got dark, it got *reeeealllly* dark. Sure, we had oil lamps and such, but the darkness overwhelmed everything. And with the dark came scary sounds of hippos roaring, jackals howling, crocodiles hissing, snakes slithering, and scorpions scrabbling. Making it through the night was scary.

In the underworld, the dark was a challenge for Ra, too. That's why twelve snake goddesses carrying torches emerge to light his way. Now he is stepping out of his day boat, Mandjet, and into his night boat, *Mesektet.* That's our signal to board, people.

As we approach Ra's boat (don't look directly

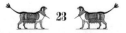

at him; he is the sun after all), you will notice the goddess Ma'at step in alongside him. As the goddess of order, truth, and justice, she is particularly important to Ra on this journey. The dark side revels in chaos, lies, and destruction, but with Ma'at next to him, Ra has the power of order and goodness on his side.

STEP UP! STEP UP!

Don't be shy! It may seem crowded with all us gods on board—including Horus, Set, Isis, Nephthys ("Hi, Mom!"), Sekhmet, Thoth, Hathor, Serket, and others—but we'll all fit. It's a magic boat. Don't expect a lot of conversation. We feel tense as Ra steels himself for battle, a battle he has waged since the beginning of time. The rest of this hour is disturbingly quiet. All we can hear is the slap of the dark water against the hull of our boat.

Do not make any sudden movements, young mortal. We don't want Apophis waking too early. Still, do you feel it? That sense of inexplicable dread emerging from the deep? The premonition that something horrible is about to happen?

He's out there somewhere: Apophis, our evil enemy, slithering toward us in the dark.

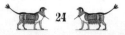

WATER WORLD
✑ HOUR TWO ✑

As we move into the darkness of the next cavern, we hear the drip, drip, drip of fetid liquid sweating from slimy cavern walls. The air reeks of rotting flesh. Apophis must have burped.

The river we are travelling on cuts through the underworld like the Nile snakes through Egypt. There is no wind, not even a trace of a breeze. We gods must do the rowing with special golden oars. And, yeah, they may look pretty, but they weigh a whole lot more than wood, which is why I'm thinking maybe *you* should be doing some of this hard labor! But no, we cannot let you. History has shown that you mortals go nuts over gold. We gods better hold onto these oars while you're around.

FLEET OF GODS

Look behind you. A fleet of boats carrying even more gods is trailing us in the dark. They are backup fighters. Not like we need their help, but it doesn't hurt to have them around. You know, just to be safe.

Once we move past the stinky entrance to this second cavern, we can relax a little. Why? Because we are moving into the region of Wernes. This, my friends, is one of the few happy places on our journey. It's where those who have lived by the rules of Ma'at and have passed my judgment (more on that later)

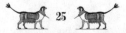

are set up for their eternal lives. Here Ra rises from the boat to dispense plots of rich farmland to the deserving dead. Ra owns the land in the underworld, just like the pharaohs owned most of the land of Egypt above. There the pharaoh assigned plots of farming land to individuals and families. This way, he could manage the land's resources, storing grain in huge silos, for example, to make sure he could feed his people in case of famine.

Fortunately famine and starvation are nonexistent in the underworld. The land that Ra distributes here is extremely fertile all year round. Plus, everything grows to magical proportions—figs the size of melons and pomegranates the size of basketballs. The wheat and barley fields are as vast as the Red Sea. It's truly a land of plenty for the dead.

Good thing, too; eternity is a *loooooong* time, people.

MAGICAL WORKERS

Ra makes sure everyone gets the same amount of land, whether they are poor peasants or rich nobles. The rich, of course, would rather not work their own fields. So they stuff their tombs with magical statuettes called *shabtis*, who will do the work for them.

Shabtis came into use after the days when only pharaohs got mummified. In the early days, pharaohs sometimes had servants killed and buried with them

to attend to their needs forever in the afterlife. After all, no self-respecting pharaoh would be caught *dead* doing his own afterworld laundry or making his own eternal breakfast.

But as you can imagine, murdering servants did not go over well with the palace staff. Eventually, magical statuettes came into being. These shabtis were carved in the form of a mummy, which indicated that they served the dead. All you had to do was point to one to make it come alive and do your bidding. Each statue was inscribed with a spell that ensured it would magically obey. The spells usually went like this:

> *Oh, shabti, if* [insert your name here] *be summoned to do any work that has to be done in the realm of the dead—to make arable the fields, to irrigate the land, or to convey sand from east to west, you shall say, "Here I am" and "I shall do it."*

Some tombs contained hundreds of these magical statuettes. Ah, magical statues that came to life to do our dirty work. Now *those* were the days!

It's time to wave goodbye to all the happy dead as they settle onto the lush plots of land that Ra has given them. Isn't it nice to be cheered as we sail by? Of course, the blessed dead are actually crying out to Ra in gratitude for his gifts—and not to us—but still.

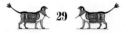

It lifts us up a little bit. We're going to need a boost as we head into the third hour.

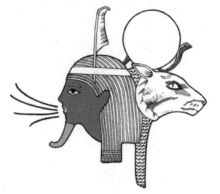

OSIRIS RETURNS
HOUR THREE

THE SOUND OF CHEERS FADES AWAY and everything goes eerily quiet again as we enter the third cavern called the "Waters of Osiris." See that mummified body on the craggy bank? That's where our night boat is headed. We will moor beside it, and Ra will summon it to life before your eyes. But don't worry. It's just Osiris, my dad, the head god of the underworld.

Osiris actually *lives* down here, so Ra isn't actually bringing him back from the dead. His summons is more of a ritual affirmation of my dad's place on the boat, and the important role he plays in battling Apophis.

EGYPT'S FIRST PHARAOH

My dad, Osiris, was an important guy, if I do say so myself. My people believed that he was Egypt's first pharaoh. He brought farming to the land and showed humans how to live like people and not animals. He achieved many great things, *me* being one of them, of course.

Osiris ruled happily in Egypt while I was in charge of the underworld. All of it. Then the jealous god Set murdered his own brother Osiris. After lots of drama—including the cutting up and hiding of Osiris's body parts—his wife, Isis, came to me for help in re-assembling Osiris's body, which I did through the magic of mummification. Then we brought the old man back to life. The catch was he could only live in the land of the dead. (Hey, you can't have everything, am I right?)

Still, let the record show that *I*, Anubis, revived and resurrected my own father. And how did dear old dad thank me for resurrecting him? He demoted me. Yeah, Dad took *my* job. He became the top god of the dead, pushing me down to number two—as mere god of judgment and embalming.

Now, I ask you, *is that fair*? I mean without me, he'd still be in pieces! But I'm not bitter. Really, I'm not.

Anyway, thanks to my magnificent mummification

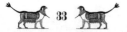

and resurrecting abilities, Osiris became the model mummy, the symbol of what everyone hoped for themselves in the afterlife—to be preserved in their earthly form and live forever. So despite the fact that he took my job, many of the prayers for the dead are aimed at me, because I'm the guy who made it all happen.

Just sayin'.

I WANT MY MUMMY!

With Osiris as their example, my people believed you needed your body to join the party that never ended: no body, no afterlife. Of course, in a pinch, your statue might do, but for the most part, people preferred a future in their own skins . . . *literally*.

So how did it all begin? When the earliest Egyptians buried their dead in the desert, the intense heat dried out the corpses, mummifying them in a crude way. My people noticed the dried-out bodies and figured that's what we gods wanted for them. Some bodies, though, were ripped apart by wild animals before they dried out. Nobody wanted *that*. So they put the dead bodies in coffins to protect them from wildlife. But without direct contact with the desert sand to bake them dry, the bodies melted into goo. That's when people began experimenting with

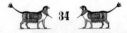

different preservation techniques. Eventually, they found the best process for preserving the dead, which went something like this:

STEP 1—PURIFICATION

After death, the body was taken to the *ibw* (eeb-oo), the tent of purification, where it was ritually cleansed and purified. The ibw was a temporary holding place, usually erected near a canal or the Nile so that all the yucky stuff could be washed away.

My priests learned quickly that when it came to mummification, moisture was not their friend. So they drained away the blood and other body fluids.

The head embalmer, known as the "Controller of the Mysteries," acted on my behalf, often performing rites while wearing a gleaming black mask of my handsome jackal face. He was my favorite.

STEP 2—EMPTYING THE BODY

After cleansing and draining all liquid from the body, the priests moved it to the *wabet* (wah-bet) or place of embalming, where the organs were removed. Left in the body, organs decay and melt into a gooey mess. Mummification and gooey messes don't mix, people. So everything that could—or would—liquefy had to go.

A priest, called a "slicer" or "ripper up," made a cut in the abdomen with a knife made of obsidian, a

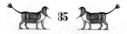

volcanic rock. Then the other priests chased him away from the tent by hurling insults and throwing rocks at him. Why? Because he had "hurt" the body. You needed your body for the afterworld, so anybody who hurt it had to be punished! (It made sense to us.)

Another priest put his hand through the cut and removed the lungs, stomach, intestines, and liver. The brains had to go, too. The priests stuck a long thin tool up the nasal passage into the brain, whipped the gray matter into liquid, then sat the mummy up to let it drain out of the nostrils. Sometimes they drained the brain through a hole in the back of the head.

Either way, fun times.

Finally, my priests popped the eyeballs out. Why? They melt too, folks. The only organ they left in the body was the heart. I'll explain why later.

STEP 3—PRESERVING THE BITS AND PIECES

Once the body was emptied, the lungs, stomach, liver, and intestines were individually preserved and placed in containers called *canopic* jars. In this way the organs would still be available to the newly reborn body on the "other side."

Each canopic jar sported the head of one of the four sons of Horus, minor gods who protected the organs. Naturally, they reported to me. Hapy, the baboon-headed god, guarded the lungs; Imsety, the human-headed god, looked after the liver; Duamutef,

the jackal-headed god, watched over the stomach and upper intestines; and Qebehsenuef, the hawk-headed god, was in charge of the lower intestines. Nail clippings, hair, and other odds and ends were often kept nearby, just in case the mummy might want or need them in the afterworld.

STEP 4—DRYING OUT THE BODY WITH SALT

The body was then packed—inside and out—with natron, a type of salt. This salt dried the body, much like the heat dried out bodies in the desert sand. Every step of the way, special spells and ritual prayers were recited. To *me*, of course.

STEP 5—MAKING IT ALL PRETTY

After drying, the body was taken to the *per nefer*, or "the house of beauty." There, the priests rubbed perfumes, oils, wine, and milk into the leather-like skin to make it easier to work with. In some eras, they stuffed linen, sawdust, and other material inside the body to "plump" it up and make it resemble the person in life. Sometimes small onions were placed in the eye sockets to make it look like the eyeballs were still there.

In other eras, my priests also poured melted resin (gummy, gluey stuff taken from plants) over the entire body, which hardened and sometimes turned the mummy black.

STEP 6—WRAPPING IT ALL UP

Finally came the labor-intensive process of wrapping it all up. Sacred amulets of protection were tucked inside the many layers of linen strips. It all had to be done right, so my priests spent a lot of time reciting prayers, hymns, and spells (again, most aimed at *me*, naturally) while they worked. It took a lot of fabric too—about five-hundred yards of linen on average. You could stretch one mummy's linen wrappings the length of about five football fields!

STEP 7—MASKS AND MORE

My priests often placed a special mask over the mummy's face. If the body was a pharaoh's, the mask was usually made of gold. If not, then it was made of linen or papyrus. Finally, it was painted in life-life colors. Masks protected the dead on their journey into the afterlife and also helped the *ka*, or spirit, recognize itself in the next world.

Many mummies were also garlanded with sweet-smelling flowers, so that the mummy could step into the new life looking pretty and smelling fine.

The entire mummification process took about seventy days.

Meanwhile, at the end of this third hour, with my dad, Osiris, safely on the boat, a flock of bird-headed gods—all wielding knives—appear and lead us to our next challenge. I like how their magical knives shine

in the darkness, don't you?

Apophis and his minions are in for it now. . . .

CORRIDOR OF DEATH
⚬ HOUR FOUR ⚬

When we enter the fourth cavern, we come to a dead stop. We've run aground. The river is gone! The water has faded away and turned to desert. This is unsettling for us because we Egyptians are most comfortable traveling on water. Deserts give us the creeps.

Still, there's nothing for it, we must get out of the boat, grab the ropes, and start towing. Dragging the boat over sand is no easy task, but it reminds me of how my people hauled the coffins of the mummified dead on sledges (sleds pulled by animals) through the deserts to their tombs.

We did not use chariots or any other type of wheeled vehicles to transport the dead through the desert, even over long distances. Want to know why?

1. Imagine riding a super-heavy bike through a desert of soft, dry sand. Too much work, right? Pulling a big chariot with a dead body in a heavy coffin would have been even worse. My people used chariots in the desert to hunt, not to pull the dead.

2. Traditionally, we used sledges pulled by oxen—or

sometimes people—to drag the dead through the desert. We Egyptians liked our traditions. If they worked, we didn't mess with them.

3. The sledge was pretty. It was often made to look like Ra's sun boat for our pharaohs, which symbolized their rebirth. The sledge "boat" started its trip on an actual funeral barge down the Nile. Then the sledge "boat" moved to the desert sands. That whole sledge-that-looks-like-a-boat-sailing-on-sand was just too cool to change.

4. Finally, my people were used to dragging heavy things on land. The Nile River is interrupted at several points by cataracts—rocky points creating white-water rapids—which are impossible to sail through. To make it past the cataracts, our sailors dragged their boats over land before launching them back into areas of the Nile where the river ran smooth again. Dragging boats over land was actually familiar to my people.

DEVILISH DIAGONAL ALLEY

s we tow the boat, the cavern starts to get even creepier. Suddenly the passageway slants and zigzags in crazy angles. Is Apophis leading us into a trap?

Wait, what is that mound over there? Oh, it's just dad's tomb, the secret place where Osiris's body rests

during the day. Well, it *was* secret, until I pointed it out to you. Don't tell anybody, okay? We can't have Apophis finding it and destroying my dad when we're not looking.

Osiris's secret tomb is the focal point for all his soul parts. Egyptians believed that humans had many parts of the soul, including the *ka*, which was like your spiritual double, your individual identity. Depicted as two upraised arms, the *ka* was the part of the soul that was nourished by funeral offerings, or the gifts people brought to your tomb.

The *ba* was the part of the soul that could travel, which is why it was depicted as a bird with a human head and human arms. The *akh*, depicted as either an ibis or phoenix, was the transfigured spirit of the soul—the part that joined the blessed dead and the gods in the afterlife. The *akh* could not die and was sometimes described as a radiant, shining being that ascended to the heavens to live with the gods.

DARK NIGHT OF THE SOUL

I n this hour, it is the darkest black of the night. I can't even see the paw in front of my face! Fortunately, four men appear to help us tow the boat. They magically turn into serpents that breathe fire, lighting our way as we trudge through the sandy zigzaggy corridor.

As we near the end of this hour, we see a three-

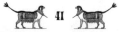

headed serpent guarding the entrance to the next cavern. Look a little closer. There are fourteen human heads popping out of the snake's body! They represent the moon's path to fullness every month.

WHY MY PEOPLE DEPICTED THE DIVINE WITH ANIMAL HEADS

The three-headed snake with fourteen human heads on its body is not so unusual. I'm sure you've noticed that most of us gods sport animal heads. And I'm sure you've been particularly admiring my noble jackal's head on my exquisitely muscled human body. Why do I have a jackal head? *The better to eat you with, my dear.*

No, I am depicted with a jackal's head for the same reason all the other Egyptian gods were shown as part beast. The ancient Egyptians understood that our greatness was indefinable and indescribable. Like the best in both man and nature, we were beyond the ordinary.

My people were keen observers of nature. After a time, they began to see certain animal behaviors as metaphors for the actions of the gods. For example, those who came to visit graveyards often saw desert jackals roaming nearby. This troubled them. Were the jackals protecting the dead? Or destroying them?

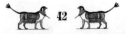

They began to see jackals as the representatives of the god of the dead—the god who had the power to both protect and destroy the dead. They began worshipping me because I had that kind of power, just like the jackals in the graveyard.

Similarly, nothing is more ferocious than a mother lioness protecting her cubs. Sekhmet, the goddess of protection, displays that kind of rage and strength. Depicting her with a lion's head was an acknowledgment of her power.

At times my people's awe of nature turned into a deep respect for specific animals. Take cats for example. (*Please. Take them. Far away from me. Seriously. I'm more of a dog person.*) My people appreciated how cats kept their granaries clear of mice. Eventually, they turned that gratitude into a special honor that saw cats as representations of Bast or Bastet, goddess of protection, pleasure, and cats (despite the fact that my cousins, the domesticated dogs, provided similar services and were infinitely less snobby, too. Just sayin'.).

I mean I loved my people, but I never understood their strange fascination with cats. And they took their passion to extremes, too, if you ask me, turning their affection into law. If a family's house cat died, everyone in the home had to shave their eyebrows as a sign of mourning. If someone killed a cat—watch out—the sentence was death. Of course, the death sentence

43

was the only part of the cat craziness that made sense to me.

The ibis was also sacred, as were certain bulls. My people were in awe of the beauty, majesty, and even danger of many creatures. They had countless animals—including falcons, cats, snakes, crocodiles, baboons, bulls, ibises, and many others—mummified and offered as gifts to the gods.

Now that you understand our god-beast natures, it's time to move on. We are nearing the end of this hour. Be sure to wave hello as we approach the three-headed-serpent-with-fourteen-human-heads-coming-out-of-its-back creature guarding the mouth of the next cavern. I'm sure glad that "lovely" monster is on our side!

THE MOUND OF SOKAR
ও HOUR FIVE ও

WE'VE REACHED THE FIFTH HOUR, and
stretching ahead of us as far as we can see is . . . yes
. . . more desert. Not good. Did I mention how much
my people detested the desert? The desert meant
death, and it's no different in this hour. Having to face
yet another hour of endless sands—tugging a *boat* no
less—may be part of Apophis's plan to exhaust and
discourage us.

But we won't give up, will we? We can't. If we
do, we'll never get out of here and the world will be
destroyed!

The going gets really rough when we have to pull

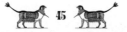

the boat up the sacred Mound of Sokar. Pulling a ship through the sand is hard enough, but now we have to drag it up a sand hill, too? Really?

Fortunately, seven gods and seven goddesses appear and take over for us. We need to reserve our strength for the battle. Meanwhile, falcon-headed Sokar, another god of the dead (not as powerful as me or Osiris, of course), soars overhead in his falcon form to protect us. His name, some think, means "cleaning of the mouth," which likely refers to a very special ceremony performed on the mummy right before it was sealed in its tomb forever.

THE OPENING OF THE MOUTH CEREMONY

After it was dragged through the desert, the mummy, in its coffin, was pushed upright at its tomb entrance. It was time for the most sacred ceremony of all—the "Opening of the Mouth Ceremony"—which made it magically possible to breathe, see, hear, and eat in the afterlife.

A special priest wearing leopard skin presided over this ceremony. Reciting spells and prayers, he touched the mummy's mouth with various instruments. One instrument was an *adze*, a small axe, made from a meteorite. My people believed we gods had sent meteorites to earth. Another instrument

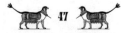

was a knife typically used to cut the umbilical cord of newborn babies.

A male bull or ox was also sacrificed. While the animal was still alive, the priest chopped off one of its forelegs and shook it—still dripping blood, I might add—in front of the mummy's face. All of these rituals strengthened the mummy's ability to come to life in the afterworld with all its senses intact.

Only after the successful completion of the Opening of the Mouth Ceremony was a mummy finally sealed in its tomb. But before everyone left, there was a great feast. Barbequed ox steaks for everyone!

After entombment, the ka was kept alive by regular visits and offerings by the family and priests, who were sometimes hired for the job. Many tombs even had "viewing slits," behind which stood a statue of the newly deceased. The slits weren't there for you to look at your relative. Instead, they were designed to let *their* ka spy on *you*! Did you bring them the good stuff? The fancy wine and bread? Or were you scrimping?

My people figured that if the dead were watching and taking notes, they'd better not take any chances. They'd better be generous. In return, family members asked for guidance from the dead. Would they help with this business situation? Take care of that nasty relative? Or make someone they had a crush on like them back?

My people believed that having the dead on their side gave them an edge in the world of the living.

YOU STARTED WORKING ON YOUR TOMB EARLY

People in the noble classes often began paying workers to build their tombs as soon they became adults. For girls that was usually about the age of thirteen, and for boys, fifteen or sixteen. Why so early? Well, if most people only lived to about thirty-five years old, then being in your teens was middle age!

Preparing for death was a full-time job. But that doesn't mean my people were death-obsessed. It's just that they loved life so much, they wanted it to continue forever. As a result, tomb building and decoration was big business.

In many tombs, just about every single inch of space was covered with brilliantly colored carvings, paintings, and murals. Some were hieroglyphic hymns and prayers (to me, of course), while others where magnificent scenes from the lives of the deceased, or experiences they hoped to have in the afterworld, such as sailing the Nile or sharing a meal with a family member. Some scenes showed domestic bliss, such as bread baking or wine making.

The pharaohs' tomb-temples often showcased great battles. Enemies were often illustrated in

chains—or beheaded. And, since my people believed pharaohs turned into gods upon their deaths, they often contained scenes of us gods welcoming them into the afterworld.

In fact, the details of the journey we are taking right now, through the caverns of the afterworld, came not from the pages of books as we know them, but from paintings. So when your little dirt-diggers (oh, excuse me, your *archaeologists*) talk about *The Book of Hours* or *The Book of Gates*, or any other "book," they're actually referring to scenes painted on the walls and ceilings of tombs; the sides of coffins; and drawn on rolled-up papyri. The same is true for *The Book of the Dead.*

In other words, there are no individual "books," people.

The Book of the Dead, in particular, refers to a *category* of writings and illustrations containing hymns, charms, incantations, formulas, spells, prayers, and amulets aimed at ensuring you made it safely into the afterworld. I should point out that whether they were written on small rolls of papyrus, or painted along the sides of coffins, their appeals were almost always directed to *me*. They were gifts of praise to soften me up.

Some people might have called them bribes. I called them my due.

The seven gods and seven goddesses who are

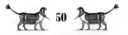

pulling us over the Mound of Sokar warn us that we will soon be sliding down the other side. We must be very careful not to lose control of the boat, especially since below us a multi-headed chaos serpent coils in wait, mouths open, ready to attack.

Thankfully Aker, a two-headed lion-man-sphinx god with a giant head on each end of his body, emerges out of the sand to help us. Wait, what is he doing? He has plopped himself over the chaos serpent. He is immobilizing the beast by, er, sitting on him. Not very dignified, but it works. After all, since Aker has two heads and *no behind*, he probably weighs more than the average one-headed sphinx. I credit this strange arrangement for Aker's ability to keep the serpent pinned down. Either that, or his breath made the monster faint.

Actually, Aker has two heads because he represents the two horizons—the one in the east where the sun rises and the one in the west where it sets.

As we near the end of the fifth hour, we can see what's ahead. Is that . . . ? Wait, could it be? Yes, it's water! We've made it through the desert!

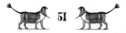

RA'S REGENERATION AND THE REBIRTH OF THE DEAD
ℒ HOUR SIX ℒ

Ah, *yessssssss*. Water. Cool, refreshing water. For us Egyptians, being on the river again is like coming home. It helps us relax, something we can do in this hour thanks to the two-headed Aker who's been sitting on the chaos serpent. Apophis, meanwhile, does not make an appearance in this hour. He's likely trying to figure out how his serpent minion was flattened by Aker.

We honor you, Aker, oh two-headed lion-man-sphinx god with no behind!

This hour is special because it's midnight—the halfway point on Ra's journey. The sun god is often described as having three phases: Khepri in the morning, Ra at midday, and Atum at sunset. The sun god's process of transforming from Atum to Khepri begins now. In doing so, he calls forth the rebirth of all the deserving dead. Plus, he unites with Osiris, imbuing him with life again.

It's a born-again bonanza.

Look at all the happy mummies high-fiving their rebirth! Let's party, people. The about-to-be-reborn are also ecstatic with relief because they passed my weighing of the heart test.

What is that test? Why, I thought you'd never ask.

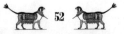

After mummification and completion of all the rites of entombment, I take center stage (finally!). I reach out a paw and call you to me. You cannot run. You cannot hide. The heart left inside your mummy—your ka spirit—*must* obey my summons. It pulls you to me like iron to a magnet.

THE ACTUAL TEST

I n the Hall of Judgment, I determine what kind of person you were and decide whether you live happily ever after, or whether to turn you into an evil, restless, tortured spirit for the rest of . . . oh, I don't know . . . *eternity*.

Fun times.

Here's how the test went.

STEP 1—PURIFYING YOUR SPIRIT

Mummification purified your body, yes, but not your spirit. So, before you dared come into my presence, you had to enter the "Hall of Two Truths" and make your negative confessions to forty-two gods. These "Declarations of Innocence" went something like this:

I have not committed crimes against people.

I have not mistreated cattle.

I have not done any harm.

I have not caused pain.

I have not made anyone to suffer.

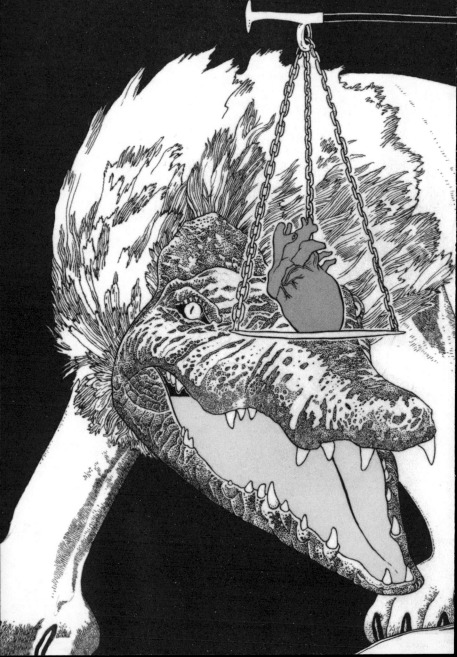

I have not stolen offerings of food left for the dead.
I have not taken milk from the mouths of children.

The confessions ended with the proclamation "I am pure, I am pure, I am pure, I am pure! I am pure as is pure the great heron. . . ."

Truthfully, these claims of purity always made me a bit suspicious. I mean, we *got* it, okay? In the end, you could say you were pure as much as you wanted and it wouldn't matter. Your heart did the real talking.

STEP 2—THE HEART GETS WEIGHED

In the presence of Osiris and Thoth, I plucked the heart right out of your chest and placed it on a scale, where it was weighed against Ma'at's Feather of Truth. The goddess Ma'at stood for order and justice. If you lived by the rules of Ma'at, then your heart weighed as much as, or less than, the Feather of Truth and you passed the test. Good for you.

But if you failed? Oh, dear. Not so much fun for you. If you lied, stole, or hurt people, your heart would be heavy and weigh more than the Feather of Truth. In punishment I would lob your twisted, dark organ to my good friend, the foul crocodile-headed demon, Amut the Destroyer. Amut has the head of a crocodile, the body of a lion, and the legs of a hippopotamus (FYI—the Destroyer is a *she*; our goddesses were

tough, but our female demons were even tougher). Once Amut devoured your heart, you were doomed to an eternity of pain and misery.

Have I mentioned how much I loved the sound of Amut's razor-sharp teeth chewing on the black hearts of the damned? There was a certain squishiness, a rubber-like smacking that really can't be found in any other type of meal. But I digress . . .

STEP 3—THOTH TAKES NOTES

Thoth, the god of wisdom and writing, recorded the results of your test in his judgment scroll. That's when we would part ways. If you passed, you went to see my dad, Osiris, who welcomed you to the land of eternal happiness and sunshine. Then you waited for Ra in the sixth hour of his journey so he could officially call you forth into living while dead.

Those that didn't pass the test—after having their hearts devoured by Amut—faced a whole 'nother world of hurt.

WHAT HAPPENED AFTER AMUT ATE YOUR HEART

The slaughtering demon-god Shezmu grabbed ahold of you next. He took the heads of the damned, and squeezed them in his wine press until they popped like overripe grapes. (Hey, don't look

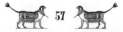

at me; they're the ones that failed the test!) However, Shezmu had a good side, too. If you passed the test, he presented you with a lovely cup of wine. There's some question, though, as to whether the "wine" he presented came from actual grapes, or the pressed heads of the bad guys. (Just kidding. He served the newly dead only the best wine, saving the blood for me.)

Then the alpha-male baboon Babi took over. Babi loved to chomp on and devour the entrails (internal organs, including the intestines) of those who failed my test. It was not a pretty sight. He ate his meals beside the Lake of Fire, which represented his rage and aggression.

If there was any part of you still left, then Sekhmet, the lion-headed goddess, tore you into tiny quivering pieces of pure misery.

See why it was so important to live according to the rules of Ma'at?

WHY THE HEART WAS KEY

The ancient Egyptians believed the heart was the seat of will, thought, and consciousness. It was where "choice" lived, and so carried the weight of a person's actions. Brains, they figured, were just stuffing to keep your pretty little head round; either that, or they were the source for snot.

The heart was so important that sometimes my

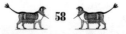

people prayed to their own hearts for help in passing
my test.

> *O my heart, which I had from my mother;*
> *O my heart, which I had upon earth; do not*
> *rise up against me as a witness in the presence*
> *of the Lord of Things.*
> *Do not speak against me, concerning what*
> *I have done; do not bring up anything against*
> *me in the presence of the Great God, Lord of*
> *the West.*

Some of you may notice that in just about every
depiction of me weighing hearts, I am shown sneakily
pulling down the chain on the side with the Feather of
Truth. Why? It made the Feather of Truth weigh more
than your heart, just in case you hadn't lived a perfect
life. Despite my steely-eyed glare, and fangs sharper
than diamonds, it turns out my own heart was a tad
soft when it came to my people.

After all, nobody is perfect, right? My people
believed that when it came right down to it, I was on
their side, which was often true. . . . Unless you made
me angry, of course.

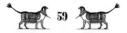

THE EGYPTIAN AFTERWORLD WAS NOT A HELL

Although there are plenty of demons and pits of fire, Duat, or the Egyptian underworld, was not a place of everlasting suffering and punishment. Those who failed my test did suffer, of course, but they didn't typically dwell in our afterworld and experience an eternity of misery. After their hearts were consumed, their heads squeezed, and their innards chomped near the Lake of Fire, they generally disappeared from our afterworld.

Good riddance, I say!

I make this distinction so that you moderns understand that while Ra's Land of the Dead may seem like a hell, it is not. Instead, it is the land through which the sun god journeys on his way to be reborn. It always has a happy ending (sunrise!).

However, during the Greek and Roman periods of Egypt's history, some stories were written that sounded a bit more like a kind of hellish place of eternal punishment. Here's one example:

Rich Man, Poor Man

ONE DAY, A FATHER AND HIS YOUNG SON heard wailing outside their window. They looked out and saw the coffin of a rich man being carried to its resting place. Great crowds of people followed the coffin,

wailing loudly. Soon after followed the body of a poor man, wrapped only in an old mat. No one walked behind him.

The father said, "The rich man who is honored with the sound of wailing is much better off than the poor man who has nobody!"

The boy turned to his father and said, "May you experience the afterworld like the poor man, and not like the rich one."

The father was saddened by his son's words, and did not see what he meant.

"Let me take you to the western desert and show you the fates of each man," the son said.

In the afterworld, the father and son entered one hall where they saw people plaiting ropes while donkeys chewed them up just as quickly as they were finished.

In another, starving people reached for bread and water hung over their heads, but people at their feet dug pits that made it impossible for the starving people to reach the food and water. In yet another hall, the corner of a door was slammed—over and over again—into the right eye of a criminal who wailed loudly at the horrible pain.

Finally, the father and son entered the hall where they saw Osiris, the god of the dead, seated on his golden throne. Anubis stood on his left and Thoth was on his right. The scale for weighing the heart against Ma'at's Feather of Truth stood before them.

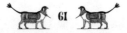

The father saw a rich man clothed in fine royal linen standing near Osiris, and was impressed by the man's status. He assumed the man was the wealthy one they had seen earlier.

His son, however, set him straight. "My father, did you not see that rich man in royal linen standing by Osiris? He is the poor man you saw wrapped in a mat. Anubis weighed his heart and found that his good deeds far outweighed his misdeeds. Osiris gave to him all the riches of the wealthy man."

"What happened to the rich man?" the father asked.

"Do you remember the criminal who had a door slammed into his right eye repeatedly? That was the rich man. When Anubis weighed his heart, his misdeeds far outweighed his good deeds. And so he suffers. Now, do you understand why I said I hope you experience the afterworld like the poor man and not the rich one?"

"Yes, my son. But now tell me—what is happening to the people who are plaiting the rope eaten by donkeys, and the starving ones with pits at their feet keeping them from reaching the food?"

"Their misdeeds were found to be more numerous than their good deeds also," said the boy. "How they lived on earth determined how they'll live in the afterworld. He who lives a good life on earth lives a good life in the afterworld," the boy continued. "And he who is evil, to him the afterworld is evil."

 62

When they left the land of the west, the father marveled at what he had experienced and learned. The boy would later grow to be a powerful magician.

RA GOES FOR A SWIM

Watch.

As Ra leaves the boat and enters the water, a serpent with five heads slithers up from the depths to surround him. But don't worry. It's not a bad-guy serpent. This giant snake is here to protect Ra. When Ra emerges from his snake-encircled cocoon, he will be closer to his rebirth as Khepri. He will be young and vital and fierce!

Ra's Khepri form is often represented as a scarab beetle. Having Ra symbolically emerge as a giant bug, by the way, is a good thing. The scarab beetle was one of the most revered and sacred symbols in Egyptian religion. My people's respect for the critter came out of their observations of its interesting behavior.

The beetle pushes a ball of dung (fancy word for poop) across the desert with its little legs. It's hard work, too. Impressed by the bug, the early Egyptians imagined that the sun was like that dung-ball, and that Ra was pushing it across the sky. Then they noticed that the scarab beetle laid its eggs inside the ball of poop. And from that ball of waste burst new baby beetles. This explosion of life from dead matter became a powerful metaphor for rebirth.

KEEP YOUR FINGERS AND TOES IN THE BOAT— THE CROCS ARE HERE

Don't be alarmed to hear the splashing of crocodiles. In this hour, Sobek, the crocodile-headed god of water makes an appearance. The Nile crocodile was one of the most ferocious predators in Egypt, weighing up to 1,500 pounds and growing up to nineteen feet in length.

It's no surprise, then, that temples dedicated to Sobek were built in almost all of the regions near the Nile where the crocs liked to snack on humans. Fishermen, in particular, prayed to Sobek for protection. But Sobek didn't always listen.

"Tame" crocodiles were often kept in Sobek's temple pools where priests decorated them with gold and jewels. Yes, my people bejeweled the beasts. Hey, it made Sobek happy to see his ugly brutes all shiny and pretty. And whatever made Sobek happy, made the crocs happy. Or, at least, that's what my people hoped.

Another fearsome creature that often attacked my people was the "river horse." You moderns call it a hippopotamus. These beasts often attacked boats, and stomped on anybody who got too near their territory.

Lucky for you, we won't see any river horses on this boat trip.

THE PHARAOH PARADE

T he people who passed my test are not the only ones regenerating in this hour. Ra also awakens all of Egypt's dead pharaohs so they can join us in combating the dark side. My people believed that pharaohs were semidivine while they ruled, and became full-time gods when they died. Once they joined the divine team, it was their job to help Ra fight Apophis on his nightly journey.

Oh, look, here they come now!

Do you see that woman over there? Yes, I said woman. Don't let the beard fool you. She wore that beard to show her kingship. Though women enjoyed more rights than in other civilizations, it was rare for a woman to rule as pharaoh. Her name is Hatshepsut, and she was a magnificent queen. She expanded Egypt's territories, improved trading, stabilized the economy, and built great monuments and temples.

She is buried in her tomb near the entrance of the Valley of Kings, which later became a popular tomb spot for many pharaohs. Decades after Hatshepsut's death, her successor had her statues toppled and her name struck from all the records. Why? Nobody knows. But she got him back in the end. Today most people know *her* name, but not his!

And look, there is Ramses the Great, who ruled for more than sixty years, and built extraordinary temples and monuments. He fathered more than

one hundred children. He also claimed that he *personally* defeated the entire Hittite army in one battle that actually ended in a draw. Yeah. Like all good politicians, the man knew how to spin a good story. However, he is most famous for coming up with history's first peace treaty. He made peace with his enemies the Hittites, so they could gang up together on an even bigger enemy, the Assyrians.

There are other pharaohs you might recognize—Akhenaten, the ruler who tried to impose a new religion with a belief in only one god; Tutankhamun, the boy king; Taharqa, the Nubian pharaoh who saved Jerusalem from the Assyrians; and even Cleopatra, the last pharaoh of the dynasty of Greek rulers.

PYRAMID POWER

There's one pharaoh, though, that you won't want to miss. Here he comes now! Khufu was one of Egypt's early pharaohs and the man who built the Great Pyramid at Giza. At fifty stories high and thirteen acres wide, his is the largest pyramid ever erected. It's the only one of the Seven Wonders of the Ancient World still standing.

Many of the stones used in the pyramid weigh more than a *car*. And yet my people cut, carved, and moved these immense stones without the use of wheels, and with only the use of hand tools such as chisels and saws.

For a long time, your people thought slaves built the pyramids. They did not. The pharaoh gave jobs to his people as a way to keep them busy during the long months they couldn't farm and had no other work. You moderns might call that a "public works" program. In return for their hard work, Khufu housed and fed them, and even paid them in oil, bread, and beer.

Buried around the pyramids were two solar boats for King Khufu's ka to use after death. Since my people believed Khufu became a god after death, they thought he might as well have his own solar boats, just in case Ra needed backup.

Each boat—measuring almost one-hundred-fifty feet long—was carefully taken apart and buried in layers in the sand around the pyramid. It took ten years for you modern geniuses to figure out how to put just one of these boats together. My people, they could build boats like this in their sleep.

Although the pyramid was supposed to be Khufu's tomb, neither his mummy nor his treasure were found inside. In fact, neither has *ever* been found. But I know where his mummy is buried. In fact, I know where to find *all* the missing mummies and their treasures your dirt-diggers are always seeking. But I'm not telling.

Why should I? Nothing gives me more pleasure than watching you people wander in clueless circles around our deserts. Seriously, I wouldn't trade that laugh-a-thon for anything.

Meanwhile, our lovely hour of regeneration is coming to its end. Ra is restored, the pharaohs of old are regenerated, and all of the blessed dead are reborn. What an hour!

But don't get too comfortable. Things are about to get *ugly*.

THE MONSTER ATTACKS!
ᘯ HOUR SEVEN ᘯ

HOLD ON TIGHT! This boat is about to start
lurching and bobbing. Apophis has slithered out from
his hiding place and, boy, is he mad. As we enter this
hour, we can see Apophis in the middle of the cavern
sucking all the water out of the river. He plans to run
us aground so he can devour Ra!

But we are not going to let that happen. The
goddess Isis throws up her arms and chants magic
words to ward off the monster. She summons a giant
snake that emerges from the water to form a barrier
of safety around Ra. We gods also encircle Ra for an
added layer of protection.

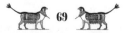

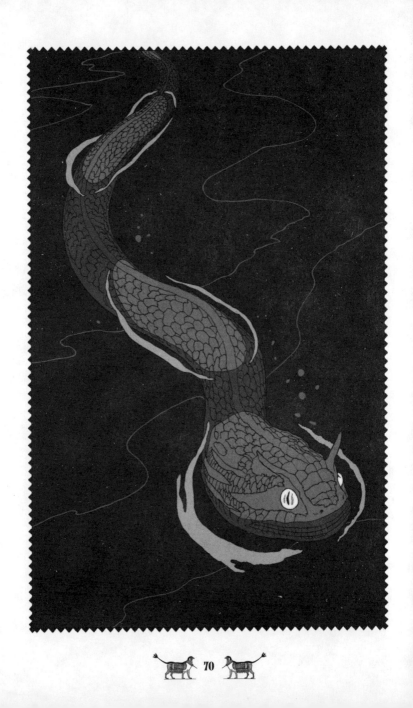

You may want to hold your nose because it reeks of rot in here and it's only going to get worse. Isis, Serket, and Set leap off the boat—shining knives held aloft—and start slashing at Apophis. The goddesses of magic and scorpions, and the god of chaos are too much for the monster. With savage yells, they carve him into huge chunks of quivering reptile flesh. (A word of advice: Never—and I mean *never*—make our goddesses angry. I tell you this for your own good because they *will* cut you. And I mean that literally.)

But even as Isis, Serket, and Set continue chopping Apophis into sushi, there is more danger. All of Egypt's enemies—those who would try to hurt, invade, or conquer us—spring up out of the ground. You might want to turn your head because we gods are about to decapitate them. We don't play. We get the job done.

Okay, you can look now. The bouncing heads are a sight to see. Did you know that after decapitation the brain still works for about fifteen seconds? If the person was talking, their mouth will continue moving. They may even continue blinking. Yeah, pleasant dreams, tonight.

Uh, oh. Apophis is beginning to regenerate! Thankfully, a giant cat goddess enters the fray and helps Isis cut him into even smaller pieces with a super-sharp knife. This might be the only time I'm genuinely happy to see a cat.

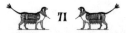

Meanwhile, twelve gods and twelve goddesses appear, each pair representing the hours of the night. Horus leads them in procession. Their star crowns shine and twinkle in this dark cave and look quite beautiful.

We think we're safe, but stay on your guard. We are never really free from Apophis. He has not finished with us yet.

You may have noticed that Isis was the first god to attack Apophis. That's because she rocked. Isis has always been fearless and strong. She was smart, fierce, and stubborn, as well as powerful. She also tricked Ra into promising that her son Horus could rule Egypt when he grew to be a man. And she did it all with cleverness and magic. Here's how Isis tricked Ra.

Ra's Secret Name

ISIS KNEW EVERYTHING in heaven and earth except one thing: Ra's secret name. Knowledge of this name, she knew, would transfer his power to her. So, of course, Ra refused to share it.

Isis came up with a plan to make Ra reveal his secret name. Ra, who had grown old, sometimes drooled. Isis collected the god's spit and mixed it with the earth. Using her magic, she fashioned a snake out of the moist dirt and made it come alive. She left the snake at the crossroads where the great god passed during his

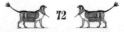

72

daily tour of Egypt.

As Ra passed, the snake sprung out and struck the god, then disappeared. Ra's cry of pain and surprise thundered throughout the heavens and earth.

"What is it?" cried the gods who had accompanied Ra on his walk.

But Ra could not answer as the poison roiled through him. He trembled violently and soon lost his sight.

He called out to his companions, "Come to me, all you gods who came into being in my body, who came forth from me. Something painful has stabbed me. My heart does not recognize it, my eyes have not seen it, my hand did not make it, and I cannot identify it in all that I have made. I have never felt pain like this. Let the children of the gods, those who know their magic spells, be brought to me."

The children of Ra gathered around him. All were at a loss—except, of course, Isis. She stepped forward and explained that she created the serpent that bit him. And only she could use her magic to cure him. But in order for the spell to work, she needed his true name.

"I am he who made heaven and earth, who knotted together the mountains and created the waters." Ra said. "I am he who made two horizons of east and west, and set the gods in glory in them. I am he who opened his eyes so that light might come into being; he who closed his eyes, so that darkness might descend. The

Nile flows at my command. My name the gods do not know. I am Khepri in the morning, Ra at noon, and Atum in the evening." The poison continued to course through his body and Ra's agony only increased.

"Nice try," Isis responded. "But you still have not given me your true name. Without it, I can't free you from the poison. Oh, and by the way, before I free you from the poison, I need you to promise that Horus will take the throne of Egypt when he comes of age."

Ra agreed. He whispered his secret name to her. Isis uttered the spell that cured Ra. The sun god fully recovered.

You could say that Isis was the world's first stage mom. She did whatever she needed to do to make sure her kid ended up as star of the show.

MAGIC AS MEDICINE

Egyptian doctors wanted a piece of Isis's magic, so they recited the story of Ra's secret name aloud to patients who had been bitten by snakes or stung by scorpions. The story itself, they hoped, was a kind of magic.

Snakebites, scorpion stings, crocodile maulings, hippopotami attacks—all these contributed to the early deaths of my people. That was the risk of the land. In the desert, you had scorpions and snakes, and on the Nile, you had crocodiles, hippos, and more

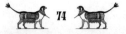

snakes. It was not an easy life.

Still, Egyptian doctors had a great deal of knowledge—thanks to me and my lessons in mummification. My priests learned to "read" the internal organs when they emptied the body, which sometimes helped them identify the cause of death as well as diagnose the living. Egyptian doctors also knew how to set broken bones, perform some types of surgery, and provide dental care.

Speaking of beautiful teeth, I notice you have been admiring my exceedingly sharp and shining canines. I cleaned my teeth the same way most of my people did. I brushed them with a frayed twig, and rubbed my teeth with a mix of natron, the salt used for mummification, and cleansing herbs such as nettle, mint, pepper, and dried iris flowers. At least I didn't stoop to what some ancient Romans did to keep their choppers pearly white. It's so gross, I can't even bring myself to write it. But I will give you a hint: did you know that human urine has bleaching properties?

Shudder.

My people also believed that knowledge of the body was only one part of healing. The rest came from Magic with a capital "M"—magic that the gods controlled, and the priest-healers tapped. Many medical papyri include magic spells and incantations for healing. Here's one for dealing with snakebites and scorpion stings.

The Priest's Spell for Healing Bites and Stings

Fail, poison. Go out from Ra,

Come forth from the burning god at my spell!

It is I who acts; it is I who have the power.

I am the one who made you; I am the one who sent you. Fall to the ground, poison.

Behold, the great god has divulged his name, and Ra is living.

The poison is dead through the speech of Isis, the great mistress of the gods, who knows Ra by his name.

It wasn't enough just to utter the spell, though. You needed specific images to call forth the magic. You had to say the words over the images of Ra and Isis. Plus, you had to *lick* an image of Horus painted on your hand. A healer-priest might also write the spell on strips of linen and place them at your throat. Sometimes, he would toss these strips into a cup of beer and, when the ink dissolved, you'd drink the mix, bringing the magic physically *into* your body.

The ancient Egyptians believed this treatment was *a million times effective* for scorpion stings and snakebites. I hate to contradict my people, but let's just say this: I enjoyed greeting the constant stream of the dead those doctors sent my way. Oh, how I do miss the good old days. But enough reminiscing. We are approaching the next cavern. Are you ready for more?

THE WEAVING OF TIME
⚘ HOUR EIGHT ⚘

Even though Isis, Serket, and Set made mincemeat out of Apophis, the water he sucked away has not come back. We are on the desert sand, which means we have to tow the boat again.

I don't know about you, but I'm getting tired of slogging through the sand. We gods are strong, but this is ridiculous. We have to keep the boat moving, though.

Apophis's minions, in the form of disgusting, slime-coated snakes, suddenly emerge out of the sand to try to bite us on the ankles. Worse, they are hissing strange words. I think they are trying to uncover our secret names so they will have power over us!

That is not going to happen. Nobody—and I mean *nobody*— knows or can guess my secret name. (So don't even bother trying, kid.)

Fortunately, a band of Ra's magical servants emerge out of the sand to protect us. They're in the form of the hieroglyphic letter for "follower" and each carries a giant curved knife with a human head hanging from each end. After we've minced and diced their leader, those slimy snakes don't dare attack us, not with these knife-wielding protectors at our side. The snakes take one look at them and slither away, disappearing into the sand.

Soon, we find ourselves moving through various

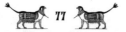

circles within the larger circle of the cavern. In one we pass a ram-headed god bearing a solar disk on his head. That is Ptah, a creator god as well as the patron of artisans and builders. We trudge past four forms of him, each one holding the symbol for linen bandages.

We also pass circles where Horus appears, and other circles where animal-headed gods sit by weaving instruments, such as spindles and looms, which have been set firmly in the sand for us to see.

THE FABRIC OF OUR LIVES

I'm not surprised to see so many symbols of weaving and linen in this hour. Linen was very important to my people. The Egyptians cultivated flax, and expertly spun and wove the fiber into beautiful material famous throughout the ancient world. The Roman admiral Pliny described a bolt of Egyptian linen as so fine, it could be pulled through a signet ring. Linen bandages, of course, were also important, because they wrapped the bodies of the dead.

My people looked down their noses at people who wore fabric made out of sheep's wool. Egyptians believed that animal hair was impure. And besides, it smelled.

This is why you would never dream of entering a temple in anything but Egyptian linen. The insult to us gods would've been too great. We would've had to

smite you. (Don't worry. We're making an exception for you and your multi-colored modern fabrics like cotton and polyester.)

Soon we enter another circle where the ancient gods of sky, air, and moisture appear on the banks to cheer us on. They plant themselves on the hieroglyphic symbol for cloth and cry out from their souls in encouragement. Their support really does help, and we find ourselves stepping a little livelier.

HIEROGLYPHICS: THE WRITING OF MAGIC

The fact that the gods we pass are sitting on a hieroglyphic symbol is important. It shows how much the "magic" of writing and reading was associated with us gods. My people essentially thought that reading was magic. Even when the Egyptians developed different forms of writing, such as "hieratic" (cursive) and "demotic," (casual writing for everyday use), they still considered hieroglyphics a sacred language. If you could read hieroglyphics, it meant you could access its sacred power and magic.

Hieroglyphics, of course, were a form of writing using "glyphs," or symbols, that we Egyptians invented. By the way, you read hieroglyphs in the direction of the faces of whatever creatures are represented. So, for example, if the symbols face

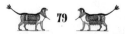

right, you have to read them right to left, just like our ancient neighbors the Hebrews and the Arameans. Below, the symbols face left, so you read the glyphs as you normally read, starting at the left.

Can you read my motto? I know you moderns need help, so I have provided a key. Here's a hint: some glyphs represent letters in the alphabet, while others represent vowel sounds.

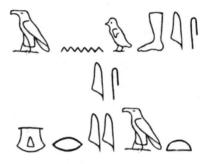

Key

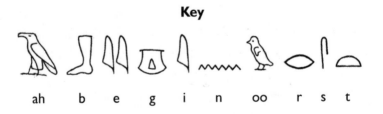

| ah | b | e | g | i | n | oo | r | s | t |

Ah, yes, say it again, please.
"Anubis is great."
Mmmmmm. Music to my ears.

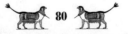

PROVISIONS FOR THE DEAD
ᔰ HOUR NINE ᔰ

WATER! YES! Now we can sail rather than trudge
through this cavern. This hour promises to be pretty
mellow, too. Do you see Ra carrying sheaves of wheat?
He's bringing food to all the blessed dead. Oh, and
look, he's bringing them clean laundry, too! Didn't I
tell you Ra was awesome?

Hopefully, most of the blessed dead don't need
these provisions. After all, in Hour Two, they got their
plots of land for endless super-food farming. Also, if
a family member or a priest regularly brings food,
wine, and other offerings, they should be fine. But we
Egyptians don't like to leave anything to chance.

My people believed in covering every possible angle. That's why they stuffed their tombs with food and drink and other goods—just in case somebody forgot their names or stopped bringing offerings. And that's why they imagined that Ra also brought provisions in the afterworld—just in case they ran through all their tomb supplies. You moderns might have called it "hoarding." We called it smart.

A FAMOUS EXAMPLE

King Tutankhamun (or Tut, as everyone knows him) isn't famous because he was a great king. He's famous because his tomb—stuffed with lots of pretty, shiny things—was discovered. That's it.

Now, to be fair, he didn't have enough *time* to accomplish much. Tut died at nineteen after ruling for just nine years. Since he took the throne as a kid, he most likely had several advisors making the big decisions for him.

Originally, Tutankhamun was named Tutankh*aten*. His father was the rogue king—Akhenaten—who tried to do away with us gods, claiming that the sun-god Aten (a form of Ra) was the only god Egyptians should worship. He even built a city in honor of this new monotheistic religion. The "aten" part of Tut's original name was supposed to prove how committed he was to the new single-god religion.

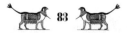

However, most of my people were not in favor of this. They worried that all the old gods would be furious with them. And, um . . . hello? We *were*. I mean, who would dare get rid of *me*?

After Tut took the throne, he changed his name to Tutankh*amun*, in honor of Amun-Ra and all of us old gods that his father had insulted. It was a way to win the people's favor, and reassure them after Akhenaten's death.

People used to think that Tut died from getting bashed in the head, but he actually died after breaking his leg, some think, in a chariot accident. The break itself didn't kill him, although it was a nasty one. The theory is that the bone broke through his skin, which let bacteria into the wound. The infection ultimately did him in.

By the way, my people used certain types of bread mold and soil mold to fight infections. The powerful antibiotic penicillin comes from bread mold. So, thousands of years before you moderns discovered bacteria and germ theory, my people were already using antibiotics. Sadly, they didn't understand how or why the bread mold worked, and couldn't make their remedies stronger.

Royal physician-healer priests likely used bread mold poultices to help Tut. But it wasn't enough. He was toast.

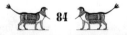

HOW KING TUT'S TOMB WAS DISCOVERED

The famous dirt-digger, Howard Carter, claimed he discovered Tut's tomb. Not quite. It was actually a kid about your age who first found the steps leading to the tomb. Carter just took the credit.

Here's what happened: It was the year 1922, according to your calendar. Carter hired many Egyptian boys and men from nearby villages to work as part of his crew. A young village boy was told to move a clay water jar. The jar had a pointed tip, which was ground into the sand for stability.

The boy did what he was told and picked up the clay vessel and moved it. But when he tried to shove the pointed tip into the sand, he heard *clink*. He figured he'd hit a rock. So he moved it. Again, he heard *clink*. And another *clink*.

That's when Carter rushed over. He brushed away the sand. The boy hadn't hit a random rock, but had discovered the top stone step leading straight into King Tut's tomb!

I, Anubis, remember because I happened to be visiting Tut's tomb on my rounds of the dead that day. I heard the clinking, followed by the excited calls and the running footsteps. And finally I heard the hushed reverent voices as light flooded my dark domain.

It had been more than three thousand years since

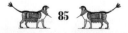

a human had taken a breath inside that tomb.

I thought about scaring the crew—maybe growling or howling—but in the end, I just inhabited my statue and observed. Eventually, Carter took everything out of the tomb, and it was exhibited at the Museum of Cairo. I was torn about this for two reasons: On one hand, I did not like it because he disturbed the final resting place of one of our pharaohs. How dare he? But on the other hand, I liked it because people the world over began speaking Tut's name. Don't forget, to us, having your name remembered was one of the ways a blessed soul could live forever. So thanks to Howard Carter, every time anyone talks about Tut, the young pharaoh's soul is strengthened, which is why, as you'll soon see, I *did not* curse Carter or anyone associated with the discovery of Tut's tomb (more on that soon).

WHAT THEY FOUND IN KING TUT'S TOMB

Like most royal tombs, Tut's had many highly decorated, painted rooms that led to the innermost chamber where his body lay undisturbed. It was also overflowing with an impressive collection of fine goods—intricately carved wooden beds and chairs; exquisite gold jewelry; several ornate versions of board games, including "Senet" (which may have been a forerunner to your modern game of backgammon);

delicate glass and alabaster jars filled with creams, lotions, and perfumes; and expertly-crafted clothing, including a pair of pure-gold sandals placed on his mummy feet. He even had chariots, in case he wanted to race his fellow dead pharaohs in the afterworld.

Tut had plenty of food and drink in there with him as well, including sides of mummified beef and gazelle meat, as well as bread, figs, cheese, wine, and more. All to make sure he would have enough for eternity.

Tut is probably most famous, though, for the golden death mask laid over his mummified body. Made of solid gold and weighing twenty-four pounds, the mask glittered with carnelian, lapis lazuli, turquoise, obsidian quartz, and colored glass. Talk about staying pretty for eternity!

Like many royal mummies, Tut's body rested inside three nested golden coffins, all decorated with scenes and spells that protected the mummy inside. Two of the outer coffins were made of wood covered in gold leaf; the third inner coffin was made of almost three-hundred pounds of gold!

The three coffins were placed inside a mummy-shaped stone casket, called a "sarcophagus," which means flesh-eater in Greek. Four shrines were erected around the sarcophagus for a total of nine structures of protection. For my people, the number nine was a symbol of infinity.

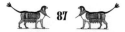

Why so much gold? My people believed the skin of us gods was made of pure gold. Since pharaohs turned into gods after death, Tut's famous mask gave him a head start.

NEWS FLASH: THERE IS NO MUMMY CURSE

The curse of King Tutankhamun is a myth. It began when the guy who paid for the discovery of the tomb died. He had been old and sick for some time. The rumor of Tut's curse got started because Howard Carter and his team kept everyone away from the tomb. The only journalists they allowed in were from one British newspaper.

In frustration, a novelist claimed she had proof of a curse. She'd made up the story in hopes it would get her in to see the tomb. As rumors and excitement grew, so did the stories about the curse of King Tut. But there was no curse.

Truth is, there are no curses at all in royal tombs. Why? Temple priests, police, and secret tunnels and chambers physically protected royal tombs. They didn't need curses. The average noblemen had no such protection, though. So they started carving warnings in their tombs to ward off thieves. Here's a real one. It is very scary so read it slowly.

> As for any man who will make a disturbance, I shall be
> judged with him.

Ha, tricked ya. It's not scary at all, is it? He's
just saying that when the thief meets me, Anubis,
at death, he will have to face my judgment. And you
know what I'll do with that evil little heart!

Now consider this one.

> A crocodile be against him in the water; a snake be
> against him on land; he who would do anything against
> this tomb; never did I do a thing against him. It is the
> god who will judge.

True, crocodiles and snakes are scary, but that's
not much of a curse, now is it? But again, I like it
because it reminds everyone that *I* will be the judge of
the thief's behavior. Yup, it always comes back to me.

During Ramses's era, noblemen's curses became
even more colorful.

> If you would do anything against this tomb,
> may you be attacked by a donkey.

Other curses claim that if you disturb the tomb,
your wife or child would *marry* a donkey that kills you.
Yeah, death by donkey . . . the real ancient Egyptian
mummy's curse. You heard it here first, folks.

THE DROWNED RISE
✹ HOUR TEN ✹

Look! The entire river is teeming and roiling with snakes. The water is so clogged with snakes and serpents you could walk across them to the other side of the river.

Go on, I dare you. Seriously. You first.

If you took me up on that dare, you might find that most of the snakes you were stepping on would help you. They're the good guys. If you haven't noticed by now, snakes can be good or evil, depending on what they do, which is why we've seen as many serpents protecting Ra as attacking him.

My people understood that good and evil were two sides of one reality. A snake in the granary that eats mice is a good thing. A venomous snake that attacks people in the marshes is a bad thing. Not knowing which one was good or bad could seem like chaos, which was scary to the Egyptians. The only way to control the chaos, they believed, was to live a good life—to live according to Ma'at's rules for justice and order.

See the two intertwined serpents standing up over there, looking like a staff in this hour? A sun disk rests on both their heads. Those snakes are clearly on our side. If not, we would be watching them trying to *eat* the sun disk—like Apophis wants to do—instead of supporting it.

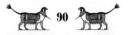

Snakes as symbols of royalty showed up on many of our pharaohs' crowns. The decoration of a cobra-about-to strike, called a *ureaus*, represented the king's power. The ureaus sent the message that the king could strike his enemies down as quickly as a snake. Also, during some historical eras, and in some parts of Egypt, my people believed that dying by snakebite automatically gave them eternal life.

And, of course, since snakes shed their skins and are "reborn" with shiny new scales, they became powerful symbols of rebirth and eternal life.

The only "all-the-time bad guy" snake was Apophis.

Watch out now! He's on the attack!

Luckily, fourteen gods step up with a magic net and throw it over the monster. Ha! He can do nothing but thrash about and hiss. This is fine by us, except for the smell coming from the monster's mouth. Think rotting fish, combined with a clogged toilet and warmed-up trash. Yeah. Dude needs a giant breath mint.

Oh, look. Here comes Horus again. He represents youth and strength and kingship. While Apophis is thrashing around, tangled in a net, Horus stretches a staff over a lake. At the bottom of that lake lie the drowned. Horus is blessing all of those who died from drowning in the Nile. They rise out of the water to live again.

His blessing was especially reassuring to the living, because the unrecovered drowned had no bodies to preserve. However, thanks to Horus in this hour, they are revived and welcomed into the afterworld for eternity.

These are the only dead, by the way, who escaped my weighing of the heart test.

The Lake of Fire and the Blood-Red Sun
♫ HOUR ELEVEN ♫

WHOA! We barely make it into this cavern before
Apophis attacks again! Get down in the boat and stay
out of the way.

Twelve gods march toward us, holding aloft a
giant snake called Mehen, the coiled one, that forms a
protective canopy over the boat. Meanwhile, our ears
vibrate with the hissing, spitting, and growling coming
from an ever-angrier Apophis, who can't sink his fangs
into Ra thanks to the extra protection of Mehen. But
that doesn't mean the monster stops trying.

Now Horus appears and then disappears into a
magic circle. He is trying to confuse the beast.

Suddenly, Horus reappears in another section of the cave holding a curved club with a snake's head carved on one end. At the same time, Set stands in front of the monster and turns into a snake himself, standing upright on his tail. Apophis is beginning to freak out.

In his confusion, the evil one hesitates. That's a mistake! In that moment we pounce on him. With Isis and Nephthy's help, we carve Apophis up like a chef wielding a set of shiny new knives.

Sushi, anyone?

It's not a pretty sight. The cavern is covered in snake blood and guts. This time Apophis is chopped up into so many pieces he can't regenerate on the spot. He will need the entire day of the sun's journey across the sky to regroup (literally).

We've done it. We've defeated the monster of the dark, the snake of chaos and destruction!

Meanwhile, Sekhmet stands in front of a large cauldron, vomiting flames into a fire pit and incinerating the heads, souls, and spirits of Ra's enemies and those who supported Apophis. The whole cavern is crimson with blood and flames. We are surrounded by the glowing color of a sun about to rise over a red-tinged desert.

One more hour, people! One more hour before we help Ra burst through the opening of the world above, into life as the newborn sun. Some of the gods are starting to sing, chant, and make noise in preparation

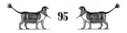

for the sunrise, for when Ra rises, it is not a silent miracle. After all, the birds, baboons, and the people of Egypt welcome him with song and celebration every day.

But let's not get ahead of ourselves. We have an interesting hour coming up. Apophis may be destroyed (for now), but we still need a mighty effort to get Ra safely through the last moments of the night.

Are you ready?

LABOR PAINS OF REBIRTH
⚛ HOUR TWELVE ⚛

You'd think that turning Apophis into sushi meant that the worst would be over. But even with Apophis all chopped up, we can still feel the tension. After all, there is no guarantee that Ra will emerge from the darkness to light the world.

We could still be attacked by Apophis's minions. Something unexpected could happen. Lots of things went wrong in childbirth in ancient times. Many mothers and infants died in the process of birth. Knowing that birth was risky for both child and mother in their world, my people assumed that Ra's morning birth was also vulnerable.

Fortunately, the priests of Ra in the city of Heliopolis stepped up with rituals to help Ra's birth along. You know, just in case chopping Apophis into sushi wasn't good enough.

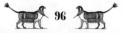

DESTROYING THE EVIL ONE ON OUR BEHALF

Before sunrise every morning, Ra's priests symbolically destroyed Apophis in many ways. First, they wrote down all of the monster's names—the names of his ka, his ba, his secret name, and his magic name—on fresh papyrus. Then they either lit them on fire or buried them.

But that was not enough for Ra's priests. They also made small wax figures of Apophis and his "agents," the enemies of Egypt, and spit, stomped, stabbed, and burned the little monsters. Then, just because they could, they urinated on what was left! Yes, because releasing your bladder on enemies is the ultimate insult and humiliation. Also, it smells.

Meanwhile, look! Here comes the great serpent Mehen to help bring us to the finish line. He descends from above us, where he has been protecting us like a canopy, and positions himself in front of our boat. Suddenly, the good-guy snake grows before our eyes, expanding to fill the entire cavern!

Ra must travel through the snake and come out of the other side to be reborn. And by *through it*, I mean *inside* through it.

Yup, all of us in the boat are going to have to slog through the insides of a giant snake so Ra can be reborn. Oh, and just so you know, we begin our journey

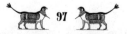

through the snake starting at its, um . . . hindquarters . . . and end by exiting through its mouth.

No, I am not joking.

WHAT? HAVEN'T YOU ALWAYS WANTED TO TRAVEL THROUGH THE BELLY OF A GIANT SNAKE?

Okay, okay. Moving through the bowels of this great snake is not entirely pleasant. I admit it. But it's what Ra needs to do in order to fully transform into his scarab beetle self, Kephri. So don't even think about trying to get out of this.

In fact, I think slogging through the gelatinous innards of this beast will be good for you. Seriously. It'll toughen you up. Take a deep breath.

Here we go!

We're now magically inside the serpent. It's not so bad, right? Well, except for the smell. And the blood. And the squishing, sucking sounds our feet make as we trudge forward.

To take your mind off the grossness of it all, grab a rope and help us pull the boat. Oh, stop complaining. The blood, guts, and gore wash off with water. Most of it anyway.

As we near the mouth of Mehen, keep your eye

on Ra. Look! He is finishing his transformation and becoming Kephri, the scarab beetle. He's so excited you can hear his giant, bug legs whirring and his sharp buggy mouth clicking in anticipation.

We are all excited because we can see the light of dawn through Mehen's open mouth. It's almost time! Ra discards his dead form like a cicada wriggling out of its shell.

We exit first, and then pull Ra through the opening of Mehen's mouth to the sounds of gods cheering, baboons chattering, birds chirping, and our people chanting. We can't help but feel excited. This is happening, people! And it's happening now.

One final tug and . . . yes! Ra is reborn. The world lives. It is lit anew!

We did it! We defeated the powers of chaos and darkness to help Ra emerge as fresh and as filled with promise and possibility as a newborn babe.

Our work here is done.

As my mummy makers used to say, "It's a wrap, people."

FAREWELL . . . UNTIL TONIGHT

Now wave goodbye as Ra sets off on his boat for his daylight journey through the sky. Don't you feel refreshed and hopeful? Watching the sunrise does that to people. It even moves us old Egyptian gods, too.

Sniff.

What happens to Apophis after the sun is reborn? He stews, grumbles, and complains, thrashing about in a rage. It will take him all day, but he will regenerate. And he will be waiting for us again tonight.

As for us gods, we go back to our day jobs. For me, that used to mean overseeing my priests as they mummified the dead and loosening up my throwing arm in case I needed to lob someone's heart to Amut the Destroyer.

But now that my people are gone, and no one worships us anymore, I have different work. These days, I hang out with my favorite mummies in the undiscovered tombs of our long-dead pharaohs.

That's right. I hang out with Snefru, Amenhotep I, Ramses XI, Akhenaten, Darius I and II (from the Persian Dynasty), Alexander the Great and Cleopatra (from the Greek Dynasty), and many, many more rulers of Egypt. I play Senet with their kas as I stretch my paws over their gleaming gold couches.

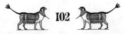

And no, I will not tell you where their tombs lie hidden. You'll have to find their treasures on your own. Cheating is, after all, against the rule of Ma'at. But, then again, if you're determined to break the rules of Ma'at, don't let me stop you.

Really. My heart-throwing arm is a little rusty. I could use the practice. And ol' Amut the Destroyer has worked up a really, really good appetite for human hearts over the millennia. She'd be happy to relieve you of yours.

No takers? Ah, well. . . . There's always tomorrow. Sweet dreams, mortals!

ANUBIS'S GUIDE TO THE GODS AND DEMONS IN THIS BOOK

Aker: Known as a primeval earth god, Aker was often depicted as a two-headed lion sphinx. He is the idolization of both ends of the horizon. (Get it? One head on each end? The two horizons?)

Amut: Sometimes called *Amit* or *Amam*, she is also known as "The Destroyer" or "The Devourer." She is my personal assistant—the crocodile-headed, lion-bodied, hippo-legged monster that eats the hearts of those who fail my weighing of the heart test. She's sweet to me, though, so I don't know what all the fuss is about.

Anubis, Me, Your Guide: Known as *Ienpw* (Yi-neh-pu) to the Egyptians (Anubis is my Greek name), I am the god of embalming and the weigher of the hearts of the dead. I determined whether you lived forever in the afterworld or evaporated into nothingness. I taught my people the sacred art of mummification. But I could be moody, too, and was often called upon to curse enemies with the blood of a black dog. (What? I like the smell of blood!)

Apophis: A giant serpent-snake demon-god of pure evil. He waits for Ra to enter the underworld at night, and then tries to devour him, thus destroying the world and all of us in it. The ultimate, nightmare-inducing, bad-guy monster.

Babi: Also one of my assistants, Babi is a baboon demon god that goes into violent rages if you fail my heart test. He will devour your entrails and throw the rest of you into his Lake of Fire, all the while screaming, baring his teeth, and jumping up and down in a rage. It's fun to watch, actually.

Bast/Bastet: A cat goddess of protection. She watched over pregnant women and loved to party with music and dance. She also protected men from evil spirits and disease. Lots of people loved and adored her. I never understood why—I'm more of a dog person myself.

Duamutef: The jackal-headed god who guarded the stomach and upper intestines of the dead in canopic jars.

Geb: An earth god who was married to his sister-wife, Nut, the sky goddess. Geb and Nut (the earth and the sky) were separated by their father, Shu, the air god.

Hapy: The baboon-headed god who guarded the lungs of the dead in canopic jars.

Horus: My half-brother, son of Osiris and Isis, Horus was the god of kingship and victory. Isis protected him from Set, who didn't want him around and fought him for the throne of Egypt. Because the gods chose Horus to succeed his father, it set the standard of succession for mortal pharaohs. Horus was usually represented with a hawk head.

Imsety: The human-headed god who guarded the liver

of the dead in canopic jars.

Isis: The great goddess/mother of Egypt, wife-and-sister to Osiris, mother to Horus and stepmother to me. The goddess of magic, protector of the living and the dead, my people called her "wise woman" and believed she had more magic than millions of spirits.

Ma'at: Goddess of truth, order, and justice. She personified the moral laws of the universe, and represented the right way to act. She was often depicted holding an ostrich feather or wearing one on her head. When the heart was weighed against Ma'at (truth and goodness), it was always depicted as being weighed against the goddess's feather.

Mehen: The great serpent that surrounds and protects Ra and his sun boat during the dangerous journey through the dark lands.

Nut: Wife of the earth god, Geb, she is the goddess of the sky. She is often depicted as arcing over the earth with stars all up and down her body.

Osiris: Ruler of the world of the dead, and my father. He civilized our people, showing them how to farm and build cities. But after being killed twice by his brother Set, he took the top post as ruler of the underworld and judge of the dead.

Ptah: Another creator god, Ptah is the patron god of artists and artisans (because they create things).

Qebehsenuef: The hawk-headed god who guarded the lower intestines of the dead in canopic jars.

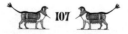

Ra: The creator god, also known as the sun god. Sometimes called Atum-Ra or Amun-Ra, Ra created himself out of the waters of nothingness and then created the rest of us gods and you puny humans. After you mortals insulted him, he left his creations to move across the sky alone, as the sun.

Sekhmet: Lion-headed goddess of rage or protection. But mostly rage. She could belch fire and rip you into threads before you even saw her coming. My people sought her out for protection from terrible events such as war, famine and disease. But her dual nature meant they also blamed her when things went horribly wrong.

Serket: Goddess of scorpions, venom, poison, and antidotes. Most often depicted either as a scorpion with the head of a woman or as a goddess with the head of a scorpion. She is whom my people called upon for help with scorpion and snake bites, and the one called on to protect the entrails of the dead during mummification.

Set: God of storms, desert, and chaos. He represented drought, pestilence, and misery. But he wasn't purely evil, even though he murdered his brother Osiris, and tried to kill Horus so he could rule. Ra liked him because Set's rage and power could be used against Apophis, the evil one. However, if bad things happened, Set would be blamed.

Shezmu: If you failed the weighing of the heart test,

Shezmu, the slaughtering demon-god, grabbed your head and squeezed it in his wine press until it popped like an overripe grape.

Shu: God of the air, Shu separated the earth from the sky. He is often depicted as holding up the sky goddess Nut over her earth brother, Geb. Shu's sister-wife was Tefnut, goddess of moisture.

Sobek: God of crocodiles, Sobek was sometimes identified with Horus as pharaoh because he could strike with vicious cruelty in defense of Egypt.

Tefnut: Goddess of moisture, Tefnut is the sister-wife of Shu, the air god; the mother of Osiris, Isis, Set, and Nephthys. I call her grandma.

Thoth: God of wisdom and writing, Thoth was associated with the moon and was sometimes called the heart of Ra. All the gods respected him for his intelligence. I did, too, I swear, it's just that I never understood why the god of wisdom was shown with a "bird brain." (Thoth is usually shown with a human body and ibis head.) Oh, and remember when I said I brought my father, Osiris, back to life? Thoth helped a little with that.

GLOSSARY

adze: A tool resembling a small axe, used in the Opening of the Mouth ceremony to ensure that the mummified person would have all of his or her senses restored in the afterworld.

akh: One of the many aspects of the ancient Egyptian soul; the akh was often identified with the individual's spirit that could influence the world of the still living.

ba: One of the many aspects of the ancient Egyptian soul; the ba was the traveling aspect of the soul, which was why it was often depicted as a man-headed bird.

canopic jars: Hollow jars decorated with the heads of the sons of Horus, where the mummified remains of vital organs were kept (the stomach, liver, lungs, and intestines).

demotic: A type of writing used by the ancient Egyptians for common documents, as opposed to more formal writing such as hieratic, a cursive form, or hieroglyphics.

Duat: The Egyptian underworld or afterworld; the place of hours that Ra must travel to be reborn with the sunrise.

embalming: The process of cleansing and preserving bodies after death, which the Egyptians did through mummification.

Giza: Archaeological sites near Cairo, Egypt, which include the great pyramids of Khufu, the Khafre

pyramids and the sphinx, and the more modest pyramids of Menkaure.

hieratic: A type of cursive writing used in ancient Egypt by priests and pharaohs, as well as the more sacred hieroglyphic writing.

hieroglyphics: A formal type of ancient Egyptian writing using symbols or pictures to create meanings or sounds.

ibw: The tent where Egyptian priests cleansed and purified the newly dead as part of the mummification process.

ka: One of the many aspects of the ancient Egyptian soul; the ka was like a person's double, the life force of the unique individual.

mummification: The process by which a deceased body is dried out and preserved.

natron: A type of salt used in ancient Egypt to dry out the body during the mummification process.

Nile River: A north-flowing river that cuts through Africa. In Egypt, the river flooded annually, after which it left rich silt for fertile farming on the river banks.

Nun: The primeval waters of abyss; the waters of chaos from which Atum-Ra and all life emerged.

per nefer: The house of beauty, where the body was perfumed, oiled, stuffed, and wrapped during the mummification process.

senet: An ancient board game dating to predynastic (pre-king) Egypt. Nobody knows exactly how it was played, but it may have been a precursor to today's backgammon.

shabtis: Small statuettes, often in mummified form, of figures that could be called upon to magically come to life and do all the hard work the deceased preferred to avoid in the afterlife.

wabet: A special room or area where priests emptied, dried, and embalmed bodies for mummification.

Wernes: Where Osiris lived; the fertile lands in the afterworld where the blessed returned to life; where Ra distributed fertile fields to the blessed dead.

SOURCES

Bolton, Ian. *Egypt: Land of Eternity*. United Kingdom. 2002–2008.
http://ib205.tripod.com/wisdom.html

Brier, Bob. *Ancient Egyptian Magic*. New York: Perennial
(reprint), 2001.

Casson, Lionel. *Everyday Life in Ancient Egypt*. Baltimore: John
Hopkins University Press, 2001.

David, Rosalie, and Rick Archbold. *Conversations with Mummies:
New Light on the Lives of Ancient Egyptians*. New York:
HarperCollins, 2000.

David, Rosalie (ed.). *Egyptian Mummies and Modern Medicine*.
New York: Cambridge University Press, 2008.

David, Rosalie. *Religion and Magic in Ancient Egypt*. New York:
Penguin, 2002.

Diodorus Siculus, *The Library of History*, Book 1. 83.5.
http://penelope.uchicago.edu/Thayer/E/Roman/Texts/Diodorus_
Siculus/1A*.html

El Mahdy, Christine. *Mummies, Myth and Magic*. London:
Thames & Hudson, 1989.

Harrison, Miranda. *Ancient Egypt and the Afterlife: The Quest for
Immortality*. London: Scala Publishers, 2002.

Hart, George. *Egyptian Myths*. London: British Museum Press,
1990.

Herodotus. *The History of Herodotus*. http://classics.mit.edu/
Herodotus/history.html

Hornung, Erik. *The Ancient Egyptian Books of the Afterlife*.
Ithaca: Cornell University, 1999.

James, T. G. H. *Myths and Legends of Ancient Egypt*. New York:
Grosset and Dunlap, 1971.

Mercante, Anthony S. *Who's Who in Egyptian Mythology*. New
York: Clarkson N. Potter, Inc., 1978.

Morenz, Siegfried. Translated by Ann E. Keep. *Egyptian Religion*. New York: Cornell University Press, 1973.

Petrie, Sir Flanders. *Religious Life in Ancient Egypt*. London: Cooper Square Publishers, 1972.

Pinch, Geraldine. *Egyptian Mythology*. New York: Oxford University Press, 2004.

Pinch, Geraldine. *Magic in Ancient Egypt*. London: British Museum Press, 1994.

Quirke, Stephen. *Ancient Egyptian Religion*. London: British Museum Press, 1992

Silverman, David. *Ancient Egypt*. New York: Oxford University Press, 2003.

Taylor, John H., ed. *Journey through the Afterlife: The Ancient Egyptian Book of the Dead*. Cambridge, MA: Harvard University Press, 2010.

Tyldesly, Joyce. *The Mummy*. New York: Barnes & Noble Publishing, 2006.

Tyldesly, Joyce. *Myths and Legends of Ancient Egypt*. New York: Penguin, 2010.

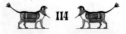

INDEX